T0194849

RECLAIMING JOY

*Living in the Transforming Power of
Reconciliation and Forgiveness*

REV. SUSAN EATON

WESTBOW
PRESS®
A DIVISION OF THOMAS NELSON
& ZONDERVAN

This book is a work of non-fiction. Unless otherwise noted, the author and the publisher make no explicit guarantees as to the accuracy of the information contained in this book and in some cases, names of people and places have been altered to protect their privacy.

WestBow Press books may be ordered through booksellers or by contacting:

WestBow Press
A Division of Thomas Nelson & Zondervan
1663 Liberty Drive
Bloomington, IN 47403
www.westbowpress.com
1 (866) 928-1240

Scripture quotations are from the New Revised Standard Version Bible, copyright © 1989 the Division of Christian Education of the National Council of the Churches of Christ in the United States of America. Used by permission. All rights reserved.

ISBN: 978-1-9736-7206-7 (sc)
ISBN: 978-1-9736-7205-0 (e)

Print information available on the last page.

WestBow Press rev. date: 09/05/2019

Contents

"...the LORD answered me and set me in a broad place."
-Psalm 118:5b (NRSV)

For my Savior
Thank you for teaching me through healing me.

Acknowledgements

When I chose to start blogging in December 2017, I never imagined I would eventually write a book. Others have encouraged me to do so for a while now, including the beautiful women of Parkway Heights UMC in Hattiesburg, MS and my senior pastor and life coach, Bruce Case. They saw something in me before I did, and helped me believe I could and should share in this way. They are a big reason this study even exists.

One thing I have been reminded of while writing this study is that I am surrounded by incredibly talented people. Thank you, Alex Doleac, for assisting me with the cover design. Your energy and excitement brought joy to my heart. Thank you for gifting your talents to this project. I also need to thank my friends who did a "test drive" of the study for me. They took the time to work the study and give me valuable feedback that was integral to its final editing. Thank you for helping me make it better than it originally was.

Finally, I need to thank my husband, Stewart, for the countless times he endured me asking for his input or patiently listened while I read portions of what I had written to him. Stewart, you are my rock, my best friend, and my constant supporter. I'm so glad I get to do life with you.

Introduction

Genesis 26 - A Case Study

When I was in seminary I was required to take a supervised ministry class. Each of us became an intern at a ministry setting of our choosing. We worked alongside the leaders, built relationships with those involved, and learned how ministry was done there. This class provided a great opportunity for self-discovery and being stretched out of our comfort zones.

The class also required us to write a case study based on an experience we had at our ministry setting. The most interesting case studies were those about a difficult person someone was working with, a conflict, or other challenging situations. We had to be honest about what happened—what we said, how we reacted or responded, what the other person or people said or did, and what the result was.

We spelled out the situation in our case study, presented it to the class, and then opened it up for discussion allowing everyone to provide their insights and suggestions. I liked this class because the learning experiences of others benefitted everyone. We all learned more about ourselves as we considered how we would respond in similar situations.

Think of Genesis 26[1] as Isaac's case study he's presenting to us, the class. As we look at this one snapshot from Isaac's life, we'll take a detailed look at his journey through the depths of fear, quarreling and opposition, as well as the strained relationships he had with the people around him. We'll journey with him through the valley, and celebrate as he enters the wide-open spaces of joy, reconciliation, and peace.

You have the opportunity with this study to comb over every detail of this season in Isaac's life slowly and deliberately, dissecting every word, every emotion, every reaction. As you learn what Isaac learned, you'll discover how you, too, can break away from these joy-stealers and live in your own broad place covered in the blessings, joy, and power of the Spirit.

It's going to be a fun ride! Let's get started.

---

[1] There are different schools of thought on how Genesis 26 fits into the rest of the narrative about Isaac, Jacob and Esau. Some scholars think Genesis 26 is in chronological order with the surrounding content. Others believe Genesis 26 is a snapshot from Isaac's past. I tend to agree with this second school of thought and have written this study with that in mind. In addition, I am not attempting to have you explore the entire patriarchal narrative. You may find that you have more textual questions concerning the greater narrative than this study will answer. I do hope you will be intrigued and inspired to study more, and encourage you to seek out studies that will help you go deeper in that respect.

Week 1 – Reclaiming Joy in the Face of Fear and Contempt

Day One: The Fear Factor

Read Genesis 26:1-5. (NRSV)

Now there was a famine in the land, besides the former famine that had occurred in the days of Abraham. And Isaac went to Gerar, to King Abimelech of the Philistines. ² The Lord appeared to Isaac and said, "Do not go down to Egypt; settle in the land that I shall show you. ³ Reside in this land as an alien, and I will be with you, and will bless you; for to you and to your descendants I will give all these lands, and I will fulfill the oath that I swore to your father Abraham. ⁴ I will make your offspring as numerous as the stars of heaven, and will give to your offspring all these lands; and all the nations of the earth shall gain blessing for themselves through your offspring, ⁵ because Abraham obeyed my voice and kept my charge, my commandments, my statutes, and my laws."

- Where is Isaac and why did he have to go there?

- Look at verse 2. What does the LORD tell Isaac not to do?

- What is Isaac to do instead? (vs. 3)

- What would be difficult about this?

- Why do you think God might want Isaac to live as an alien?

Is it possible that God is positioning Isaac in a challenging situation so that trusting God was a day-to-day necessity? Living as an alien in a foreign land in the middle of a famine would do that. Perhaps there were some attitudes within Isaac God knew needed addressing. Hold that thought, and let's keep going.

- What promises do you see God making to Isaac?

- What traits about God stand out to you in verses 1-5? In other words, what can you understand about God's character based on these verses?

Read Genesis 26: 6-11

> [6] *So Isaac settled in Gerar.* [7] *When the men of the place asked him about his wife, he said, "She is my sister"; for he was afraid to say, "My wife," thinking, "or else the men of the place might kill me for the sake*

of Rebekah, because she is attractive in appearance."
8 When Isaac had been there a long time, King Abimelech of the Philistines looked out of a window and saw him fondling his wife Rebekah. 9 So Abimelech called for Isaac, and said, "So she is your wife! Why then did you say, 'She is my sister'?" Isaac said to him, "Because I thought I might die because of her." 10 Abimelech said, "What is this you have done to us? One of the people might easily have lain with your wife, and you would have brought guilt upon us." 11 So Abimelech warned all the people, saying, "Whoever touches this man or his wife shall be put to death."

Look at verse 6.

• What trait do we discover about Isaac from this verse only?

Look at verses 7-11

• What traits do we discover about Isaac from these verses?

Isaac was obedient to be where he was supposed to be; however, fear was robbing him of joy while he was there. Instead of being at peace with himself, with God, and with others, Isaac was living in constant stress and anxiety. As a result of living in fear, Isaac jumped to the worst possible scenario about Abimelech and the other Philistine men, lied to protect himself, put Rebekah at risk, and created tension between himself and the people around him.

Can you relate to Isaac? I know I can. I have plenty of experience following God in obedience, willingly going where He was calling me, yet living in fear once I got there—fear of failure, fear of what others thought of me, fear of rejection, and on and on. But no matter how obedient I was to be where I was supposed to be, as long as I held on to fear I was robbed of the *joy* of living in the place God had brought me.

"Forgetting" the promises of God, my fear caused me intense stress and anxiety. When I acted and reacted out of that fear, it created friction between myself and others. A crucial step to reclaiming joy is getting real about the fear in our lives and taking an honest look at how it is affecting us and the people around us.

- What are some signs that someone might be living in fear? Take a moment to write some things down.

Here are some things I came up with:

- People-pleasing
- The need for approval
- Being overly concerned about what others think
- Not pursuing dreams because of the fear of failure, fear of success, fear of what others will think of you, etc.
- Living in a defensive posture towards the people around you
- Greed
- Trouble receiving feedback from others
- Unable to celebrate the accomplishments or successes of others
- The inability to be authentic and vulnerable with others.
- Perfectionism

I could go on and on, but here's the bottom line: fear is not our friend. It is a liar and a thief. It robs you of joy and doesn't produce positive results for you. As I looked again at Genesis 26:1-11, I saw seven distinct results of living in fear.

SEVEN NEGATIVE RESULTS OF LIVING IN FEAR

(BASED ON GENESIS 26:1-11)

1) Fear makes us selfish.

When we're fearful, self-preservation is our priority. When self-preservation is the priority, our decisions and reactions are more likely to have negative results on the people around us. Why? Because we are putting our interests before the interests of others.

2) Fear makes us unwise.

When we're caught up and living in fear, all our decisions are filtered through a fearful perspective. Fear, however, is based on lies, so any decisions coming from a place of fear are going to be unhealthy, unwise, and even potentially destructive to ourselves and the people around us.

3) Fear deceives us and makes us liars.

Fear deceives us into thinking that our selfish actions won't cause a negative impact on the people around us. We may lie to ourselves about the ramifications of our actions and do things we normally wouldn't do. We may lie to others to protect ourselves from what we're afraid of.

4) Fear gives us a distorted view of reality.

Fear causes us to see one, terrible ending to difficult circumstances or relationships. Every interaction, event, or conversation, when filtered through fear, becomes distorted in our minds. This distorted view intensifies the urge to take a defensive posture with others. It prevents us from hearing the truth and closes us off to the possibilities that exist with God.

5) Fear gives us "amnesia."

Look again at Genesis 26:3-5. Is there something important Isaac has forgotten? Yes! He has forgotten the promises of God! Fear can cause us to "forget" the promises of God and how God has been faithful and worked in our past for good.

6) Fear leads us to make assumptions about others.

7) Fear causes relational problems between ourselves and the people around us.

We'll spend a little more time on those last two points tomorrow. As we wrap up today, take some time to talk to God about the fear that may be present in your life. Be honest with yourself and with God always remembering how much He loves you and wants you to be free from anything that would keep you captive.

⟡ ✺ ⟡

Take some time to prayerfully consider some of your current relationships and attitudes. You can do this all in one sitting, but don't feel like you have to. You may want to take more time to think about a particular question. Take as much time as you need. The most important thing is to do it honestly.

- Where might fear be overly active in your life right now?

• Can you name any recent decisions, conversations or actions of yours that were fear-based? If so, list them below or in a journal by naming the action, and what fear was associated with that decision, comment, etc.

• How might fear be distorting the truth for you about a current situation, person, or relationship?

• Write a prayer to God confessing your fears and any fear-based actions or attitudes that are present in your life right now.

Day Two: You Know What They Say About Assuming

Read Genesis 26:9-11

> ⁹ *So Abimelech called for Isaac, and said, "So she is your wife! Why then did you say, 'She is my sister'?" Isaac said to him, "Because I thought I might die because of her."* ¹⁰ *Abimelech said, "What is this you have done to us? One of the people might easily have lain with your wife, and you would have brought guilt upon us."* ¹¹ *So Abimelech warned all the people, saying, "Whoever touches this man or his wife shall be put to death."*

- What was Isaac's reasoning or justification for lying to Abimelech?

- Who did Isaac think would kill him?

In his fear, Isaac assumed that he knew what Abimelech was thinking, what he would do and why. In our narrative, however, we see a discrepancy between the assumptions Isaac made and reality.

- How have Abimelech and the Philistines acted so far in our Genesis 26 narrative? (see verses 8-11)

- What qualities do you notice about Abimelech based on how he responded to Isaac concerning Isaac's lie?

Neither Abimelech nor his men touched Rebekah the entire time Isaac lived in Gerar, and we're told he lived there "a long time." In addition, Abimelech went to Isaac with his concerns and questions. He didn't brood silently. He didn't walk around gossiping about Isaac, dragging his name through the mud. He took his concern straight to Isaac.

From Isaac's fear-based perspective, lying to Abimelech was the right choice to save his own skin. From Abimelech's view, the repercussions of that lie on himself and his kingdom could have been devastating. He believed that if any of the Philistine men had taken Rebekah into his home and slept with her, it would have brought great guilt and disastrous consequences upon them all. Therefore, he told his men never to touch Rebekah or else be put to death.

Why would Abimelech take such drastic measures to ensure no one touched Rebekah? To answer that we need to take a look at Genesis 20:1-18

Look up and read Genesis 20:1-18.

- What did Abraham do?

- What did Abimelech do?

- What happened to Abimelech as a result?

• What was Abimelech's response to God?

• What was Abimelech's response to Abraham?

• What was Abraham's answer to Abimelech? (verse 11 only)

Abraham's assumptions about Abimelech caused him to come to a faulty conclusion and then make a selfish decision based in fear that had negative repercussions on Sarah, Abimelech, and everyone in Abimelech's kingdom.

• How would you characterize Abimelech based on what you've read so far?

❧

Have you ever noticed how we tend to cast people into categories of "good guys" and "bad guys?" "Good guys" are people who look like us, believe like us, think like us, dress like us, etc. "Bad guys" are people we don't know, we don't understand, who disagree with us, who come from a different culture, have a different belief system, etc. But do we really know who someone is or what they will do based on where they are from, what their political views are, or what their socioeconomic status is?

- What are some problems that result when we make assumptions about people we don't really know, casting them into categories of "good guys" and "bad guys?"

This tendency to make assumptions and categorize people this way can also impact the way we read Scripture, making it easy to set certain people up to be the "good guys" and others up to be the "bad guys." Take our Genesis 26 passage as an example of how we might do this:

Isaac: son of Abraham, child of the promise = Good Guy

Abimelech: Philistine, God did not make
a covenant with him = Bad Guy

Setting up good guys and bad guys doesn't always work well when it comes to reading Scripture, because, in reality, the only truly good guy is Jesus. Everyone else is flawed, broken, and messed up. No one else has it all together—not even the ones with whom God made covenant promises. To paraphrase the Apostle Paul in Romans 3:23, we're all bad guys; we've all fallen short of the glory of God. As it pertains to Isaac and Abimelech, maybe Abimelech wasn't such a bad guy. In fact, he may have been the one operating with the most integrity.

- Have you ever made an assumption about someone? Have you ever come to a conclusion about the kind of person they must be, or about what their motives are for believing or acting a certain way without really knowing them?

- Can you think of a time you made an assumption about someone and discovered later that you were wrong? If so, what did that experience teach you?

- Where might you currently be making assumptions about a particular person or people? Do your best to think of specific people and reasons for your assumptions.

Saying we should be careful about making assumptions about others is not to say that we should check our brains at the door and fail to use wisdom in our relationships. Throughout our lives, we will encounter people with whom we'll need to employ caution and good boundaries. These are healthy methods of relating. However, when we make assumptions and think we know all there is to know about people and outcomes, we take control from God and close ourselves and those relationships off to the beautiful possibilities that exist with Him.

God is the only one who knows the hearts and minds of every person. God loves you and has your best interest at heart. Equally important to remember: He loves and has the best interest of everyone else at heart as well. Rather than living from a posture of fear and assumption-making, God is calling each of us to trust Him with all of our relationships and circumstances—even the most difficult ones.

- Into what relationships and circumstances do you need to invite God? Where do you need to trust him today?

"No one is only an unvarnished lump of bad."
~ Dallas Willard

Day Three: An Ugly Little
Attitude Called Contempt

In March of 2019, the New York Times ran an article by Arthur C. Brooks entitled *Our Culture of Contempt* excerpted from his book *Love Your Enemies*. In it, he talks about something researchers call **motive attribution asymmetry**—the assumption that your ideology is based in love while your opponent's is based in hate. **Motive attribution asymmetry** is dangerous because believing your foe is motivated by hate leads to a nasty little attitude called **contempt.**

> *Motive attribution asymmetry doesn't lead to anger, because it doesn't make you want to repair the relationship. Believing your foe is motivated by hate leads to something far worse: contempt. While anger seeks to bring someone back into the fold, contempt seeks to exile. It attempts to mock, shame, and permanently exclude from relationships by belittling, humiliating, and ignoring. So, while anger says, 'I care about this,' contempt says, 'You disgust me. You are beneath caring about.*[1]

Contempt is dangerous, destructive and divisive, and it is running rampant in our culture right now. Social psychologist and relationship expert, John Gottman, documents the destructive power of contempt in his work studying thousands of married couples. He calls contempt "sulfuric acid for love," and points out that couples who constantly battle die twenty years earlier, on average, than those who consistently seek mutual understanding.[2]

This is how nasty and terrible contempt is: Contempt doesn't just destabilize our relationships, "it actually causes a comprehensive degradation in our immune systems.

[Contempt] damages self-esteem, alters behavior, and even impairs cognitive processing."[3] The American Psychological Association documents that "the feeling of rejection, that is experienced by someone after they have been treated with contempt increases anxiety, depression and sadness."[4]

This is not just bad news for the person being held in contempt; the contemptuous person is also damaged. Whenever we hold onto contempt, our bodies secrete two stress hormones—cortisol and adrenaline. When these stay in our systems for a prolonged time, they can do serious damage to our bodies.

The bottom line is this: Contempt is horrible for you. It makes you unhappy, unhealthy, and it even makes you unattractive to those who agree with you.[5] Contempt will wreck your relationships and harm your health. It also makes compromise and progress impossible between people. Are you getting the picture? Whether it's public or personal, contempt is causing significant harm.

And yet, what do we see and hear over and over again on the news, on social media, and in personal conversations with others? We hear, and possibly participate in, a lot of contempt. Whether we are talking about our current political opinions, a situation going on in the Church, an ex-spouse, a current spouse, a child, a boss, the lady at the DMV, or people we have never met but think we know what they must be like, many of us are guilty of contempt. Not simple frustration with others, but talking about another person, treating another person, or thinking about another person like they were less worthy of our respect and, yes, our love.

What are some indicators that you may be holding an attitude of contempt toward someone? According to John

Gottman, indicators of contempt include sarcasm[2], sneering, hostile humor, and, worst of all, eye-rolling. Gottman claims: "These acts effectively say, 'You are worthless,' to the other person. Want to see if a couple will end up in divorce court? Watch them discuss a contentious topic, and see if either partner rolls his or her eyes."[6]

RECLAIMING LOVE

If we are going to be men and women who are filled with the joy of the Holy Spirit, we must avoid contemptuous attitudes, behaviors, and talk at all costs, and allow the Holy Spirit to fill us with His love, becoming men and women of love. Notice I didn't say men and women *who* love, but men and women *of* love. We must humbly open ourselves to the Holy Spirit and embody love, becoming people who are so full of the love of God that loving actions toward the people around us come naturally. Love truly is the only thing radical enough to break us out of the fears we live in, the assumptions we make about others, and the attitudes of contempt we hold.

Please understand that the love we're talking about is not based on emotions. This isn't about feeling loving, necessarily. Also, we're not talking about simply acting in loving ways. Of course, acting in loving ways is part of it, but what's going to be most helpful for us to understand is love—not as a feeling, not as simply an action—but love as the *source* of our action and the *source* of our feelings.

John tells us in 1 John 4:16 that "God is love." Dallas Willard, in his book *Life Without Lack,* says "that is not an explanation of who God is; that's an explanation of what love is."[7] In other

---

[2] 1570s, sarcasmus, from Late Latin sarcasmus, from late Greek sarkasmos "a sneer, jest, taunt, mockery," from sarkazein "to speak bitterly, sneer," literally "to strip off the flesh," from sarx (genitive voice) "flesh," properly "piece of meat," "to cut" (cf.

words, I know what love is by looking at God, and I see God most clearly in the person of Jesus Christ.

Look up John 5:19 and write it here:

Whatever He saw the Father doing, that's what Jesus did. Everything he did was in love. He didn't have a mushy, warm-fuzzy feeling of love, and he didn't simply do loving actions. Jesus embodied love. He connected to the source of love, the Father. He let the Father fill him, and remained open allowing the Father to guide and direct every single thought, attitude, and action. This is how Jesus was able to love so radically. He was sourced by the Father's love, and he practiced loving God and others every single day.

Look up and read 1 Corinthians 13:4-8

We've heard these verses a lot, especially at weddings. Therefore, we may be so familiar with these words that they have lost their impact. Take a moment to read this excerpt from Dallas Willard's book *Life Without Lack* and see if it doesn't help you gain a slightly different perspective on this familiar passage.

> *"When we read 1 Corinthians 13, it's important to understand that Paul is not issuing commands; he is not saying that WE ought to be patient, kind, humble, and so forth. He is describing love as having these characteristics. That, after all, is what the passage actually says. So we 'pursue love' by advancing our faith and dying to self through appropriate training and practice, and the love we receive from God takes care of the rest. These virtues arise from an overall disposition of love, because love, by its very nature,*

> *seeks what is good and right before God…In the deepest sense, love is not something you choose to do; it is what you become—a loving person."*[8]

- Is this a new way of thinking about love for you? How so?

- In what ways did Jesus embody the characteristics of love found in 1 Corinthians 13? Name as many instances you can remember from Scripture. Feel free to search the Gospels to find more.

Our goal as men and women who choose to follow in the footsteps of Jesus is to open ourselves up to God, the source of all love, and allow Him to fill us with His love. We "pursue love by advancing our faith and dying to self through appropriate training and practice." As we allow ourselves to be filled with the love of God through drawing near to Him and giving him access to the most intimate parts of who we are, He forms us into the kind of people who are able to truly love the people around us—even our enemies.

Read Luke 6:27-38

- What is challenging about Jesus' words here? Be specific. Name the challenging statements.

- Do you believe this kind of living is possible? Why or why not?

1 John 4:18 says "…perfect love casts out all fear."

- Where fear makes me selfish and self-focused, **love makes me others-focused.**
- Where fear focuses on self-preservation, **love focuses on death to self.**
- Where fear makes me a liar, **love makes me a truth-teller.**
- Where fear makes me unwise, **love makes me wise.**
- Where fear distorts the truth, **love reveals the truth.**
- Where fear damages my relationships with others, **love heals and strengthens my relationships.**
- Where fear leads me to hold others in contempt, **love leads me to look at what is valuable in every individual.**

Fear, contempt, and love cannot co-exist in the same space. The choice is ours concerning which to nurture. Therefore, if we are going to truly reclaim joy in our lives, we must not only be honest about the fear in our lives, we must also RECLAIM LOVE.

So how does this relate to Isaac? Living in a foreign land under stressful conditions revealed the true state of Isaac's heart. Acting out of fear, his decisions could have resulted in devastating consequences for many other people. Because Isaac lied to Abimelech, distrust and animosity were created between them. **Even though Isaac was in the physical space God called him to be in, he was nowhere near the spiritual space God needed him to occupy.**

What was true for Isaac is true for us. God not only wants us to be where He calls us to be, He also wants us to occupy a spiritual space of openness and trust in Him where we can fully experience His joy and blessings, and where His blessings and love can flow through us to others.

☙ ❧ ☙

- Think about a relationship that is difficult for you right now. What adjectives would you use to describe your feelings, attitudes, and actions regarding this person/people? (Be as honest as you possibly can here—even if it's ugly.)

- Now consider what would change about your current feelings, attitudes, and actions if you chose to reclaim love for this person/people?

- How might the relationship change if you chose to reclaim love?

- Write a prayer to God asking Him to help you become a person of Love.

Week 2 – Reclaiming Joy in the Midst of Valleys, Quarreling and Opposition

Day One: Promises and Blessing

Read Genesis 26:12-14

> *¹² Isaac sowed seed in that land, and in the same year reaped a hundredfold. The Lord blessed him, ¹³ and the man became rich; he prospered more and more until he became very wealthy. ¹⁴ He had possessions of flocks and herds, and a great household, so that the Philistines envied him.*

• What do you think about the fact that Isaac has exhibited a significant lack of trust in God, and yet is prospering and has become wealthy?

During last week's study, we saw Isaac living in fear to the detriment of his relationships with the people around him. So far he hasn't looked like a man trusting in the promises of God, or someone who is letting God lead. He's been acting out of fear, taking control, and calling the shots himself. Yet, what we see today is that prosperity and abundance are all over his life! Here's the crucial takeaway:

God's promises for Isaac have not been negated because of Isaac's fears, imperfections, and bad decisions.

God made promises to Isaac saying, "I will bless you," and He has. However, God is up to something much bigger than making Isaac a wealthy guy for his life-span. Remember, God has already promised Abraham that he will be the Father of many nations, that he will be exceedingly fruitful, and the land where he was currently a foreigner will belong to his descendants. Kings will come from him. The whole world will be blessed through him (Genesis 12:1-3; Genesis 15; Genesis 17). God has reiterated these same promises to Isaac saying that He will fulfill the oath He made with Abraham through Isaac (Genesis 26:3-5).

There will be consequences for Isaac's poor fear-based decisions, as we'll see, but the promises of God remained. In other words, *Isaac isn't earning the promises and the blessings of God. They are a gift of grace.* God is going to work through Isaac's life, as flawed and full of imperfections as he is, because He promised that He would. And God is always faithful to His promises.

Envy and Jealousy

Read Genesis 26:14-16

> [14] *He had possessions of flocks and herds, and a great household, so that the Philistines envied him.* [15] *(Now the Philistines had stopped up and filled with earth all the wells that his father's servants had dug in the days of his father Abraham.)* [16] *And Abimelech said to Isaac, "Go away from us; you have become too powerful for us."*

- What underlying attitudes or emotions do you hear in Abimelech's statement, *"Go away from us; you have become too powerful for us?"*

What I hear is, *"We don't trust you!"* Was Abimelech wrong to say this? Maybe not when we consider how Isaac lied to him. Trust was not the defining characteristic of their relationship, to say the least. Isaac was becoming wealthy and his household was growing in number so that Abimelech, along with all the Philistines, felt threatened. His solution: *"Go away."*

- Have you ever been pushed out by someone who was threatened by you? If so, how did you react?

- Is there anything you would do differently? If so, what?

While Isaac had not proven himself trustworthy in the past, that didn't justify the unhealthy attitudes and actions from the Philistines. One unhealthy attitude we see from the Philistines is envy. They envied Isaac because he was prospering and becoming strong.

Depending on which translation you are reading, you'll see either the word "envy" or the word "jealousy" in reference to the Philistines' attitude toward Isaac. Have you ever thought about the difference between these two words? They seem to be used interchangeably at times, but they have slightly different meanings.

Envy is the emotion of coveting what someone else has.

Jealousy is the emotion related to the fear that something you have, or something you want to have, will be taken away by someone else.

Whichever word is used, this truth remains: neither of these attitudes is based on anything good or holy and often lead to other unhealthy attitudes or actions. The action accompanying the Philistines' envy was breaking the covenant Abimelech made with Abraham (Genesis 21:22-34) by stopping up all of Abraham's wells.

༄ ༓ ༄

- Have you ever treated someone poorly because you were envious or jealous of them? (Put-downs, deliberately not celebrating their accomplishments, ignoring them, talking poorly about them to others, etc.)

- Have you been on the receiving end of someone else's envy or jealousy?

- How did they treat you?

- What emotions did you notice rising in you as a result of that treatment?

- Make a list of results you've seen because someone was jealous or envious of someone else.

- Now, take some time to make a list of all the things you are grateful for. Appreciate what you have, who you are, and what God has done for you. Take your eyes off what you think is lacking, and give God praise for the abundance you have.

Day Two: Into the Valley

Genesis 26:17-18

> *[17] So Isaac departed from there and camped in the valley of Gerar and settled there. [18] Isaac dug again the wells of water that had been dug in the days of his father Abraham; for the Philistines had stopped them up after the death of Abraham; and he gave them the names that his father had given them.*

• What part of Gerar is Isaac in?

The word "valley" is defined as "a broad depression between two hills." It can also mean "a low point or interval in any process, representation, or situation; any place, period or situation that is filled with fear, gloom, foreboding, or the like, i.e., the valley of despair."[9]

Valleys represent seasons when it's difficult to see how things will work out, times when we feel depressed or low, or when circumstances just aren't going in the direction we would like them to go. While being in a valley typically represents being faced with a challenge or difficulty, valleys can also be places where our hope is restored, where comfort is given, and where we begin to see a way forward.

We can enter valleys for any number of reasons. Circumstances out of our control can lead us into a valley. Sometimes we enter a valley because of the choices we make, or because of what others have done or are doing to us. Other times we enter valleys due to spiritual opposition. Whatever reason you find yourself in a valley, *it doesn't have to be a place of despair.* The valley can be a place where you begin to do the hard work that will set you up to live and thrive in ways you've never known before.

- Look up and read **Psalm 84:5-7** in several different translations, if possible. Read these verses with a keen awareness of their spiritual meaning.

- According to verse five, who are the ones that are "blessed", "happy", "filled with joy?"

- What is the name of the valley mentioned in verse six?

- What types of transformation do you see in these verses? Write down the different transformations you see.

☞ ᲛᲔ ☜

Those the Psalmist says are blessed, happy, or filled with joy, are those who find their strength in the Lord and have their hearts and minds set on journeying into His Presence. This journey, however, is not without struggle. This Psalm names a valley that the people of God go through on their journey to Jerusalem. The name of the valley is "Baca" or "Weeping."

Notice that the Scripture says, *"As they go through ..."* or *"When they walk through* the Valley of Weeping..." not *"If they go through* the Valley of Weeping." Our journeys consist of valleys. There is no way around it. But the ones who find refreshment and blessings, even in the midst of the valleys, are the ones who choose to find their strength in the Lord and keep their hearts and minds set on the Presence of God. For them the valley will become a place, not of defeat and anxiety, but where they experience transformation and grow stronger.

Notice, for example, how the valley of Weeping is transformed. As the people of God journey through the Valley of Weeping toward the Presence of God, their tears of mourning are turned into springs that create an oasis. What an image! According to the Word Biblical Commentary, this is "a classic statement of faith *which dares to dig blessing out of hardships.*"[10]

As I thought about this, I considered my tendencies in the midst of valley experiences. When I first enter a valley, my tendency is to focus more on the valley than on the Presence of God. When circumstances are difficult, when relationships are strained, when I'm stressed and hurting, those things dominate my focus. But when I shift my gaze—when I lift my eyes and focus on the Presence of God—I am quickly comforted by Him. Circumstances do not immediately change, but I am strengthened and prepared for whatever the valley brings my way.

- Think about a valley you have been through or are currently experiencing. What would you name that valley? (ex., The Valley of Weeping)

- Is it natural for you to focus on God and His Presence in the midst of your valley experiences? If that is a challenge for you, what makes it difficult?

- Can you see how God has transformed or is transforming your valley into a place of blessing? If so, how?

- If you can't, what is making that hard to see?

- Name some ways your valley experiences have made you stronger.

- How can you better partner with God to dig blessing out of your hardships? In other words, what are some practical steps you can take to help you fix your gaze on God and find your strength in him in the midst of your valleys?

Day Three: Unstopping the Wells

The Valley of Gerar was both a literal and figurative valley for Isaac. He was pushed into this valley by the people he was in conflict with. Forced to leave the place where he was prospering and thriving, Isaac had to reestablish his entire family in a new location. Even though he found himself in circumstances he never would have chosen, it was in the valley that Isaac noticed something crucial: His father's wells needed to be unstopped. Faced with this new challenge, Isaac got busy doing the necessary work he discovered there. He began unstopping the wells and renaming them the names his father, Abraham, had given them.

Unstopping the wells was crucial for two reasons:

First, If Isaac were to survive in this valley—and even potentially thrive—he needed those wells open. So, on one level, there was an extremely practical reason Isaac unstopped the wells. He just couldn't live without water.

Secondly, remember, God had promised Abraham and Isaac that this land would be theirs. Unstopping the wells was not just crucial to Isaac's life in the short-term, it was also crucial to God's overall plan of establishing this family in this space for many generations.

While he never would have chosen to enter that valley, it was only in the valley that Isaac was able to see what he needed to see.

Sometimes it's not until we enter our own valleys that we "wake up" and become aware of wells that need to be opened and renamed in our lives. For instance, a valley of financial stress can reveal a stopped-up well of trust in God's sufficiency. The work of unstopping that well could be asking and trusting God for daily bread, thanking him for even the small provisions that come, being generous in the midst of the strain, waiting patiently for God to act on your behalf, and sharing your story of God's provision with others.

A valley of depression may reveal a stopped-up well of hope. The work of unstopping that well could be to read God's word daily, focusing on the statements and promises in which our true hope lies. It may include talking to others who've gone through that same valley and come out on the other side.

Perhaps the enemy has not only stopped up certain wells but given them new names as well. Maybe he has named your well of sufficiency, "scarcity." Maybe he has named your well of hope, "hopelessness." *Whatever wells the enemy has stopped up, do the necessary work of unstopping your wells—confidently renaming them the names your Father gave them.*

You don't have to wait for a valley experience to begin the work of unstopping your wells. You can do this introspective and prayerful work anytime. In fact, I encourage you to make it a daily practice with God. This prayerful, interior work is necessary because we can't thrive without open wells. To be properly nourished, even in the valleys, we must do the work of unstopping the wells.

- What wells need to be opened in your life? Name them below. (i.e., a well of trust; a well of hope)

- What names has the enemy given them?

- What steps can you take to begin unstopping those wells? In other words, in what ways do you need to "dare to dig?"

(This may include talking to a pastor, finding a counselor, or talking to another trusted friend; making an apology or accepting an apology, etc.)

One thing Isaac "forgot" in the midst of his fear was who he was. He was a child—no, he was THE child—of the Promise. Isaac was the child promised to Abraham and Sarah in their old age *(Genesis 17: 1-8; 15-22; Genesis 18: 1-15; Genesis 21: 1-7)*. His very existence in the world proclaimed, *"God is faithful to keep His promises!"* Isaac forgot this in the face of his fears. He forgot who he was, and, in a way, forgot who God was—what God was capable of and what God had promised to do. The valley took Isaac on a journey of rediscovering God's promises and his own identity as the child of those promises.

By doing the work in the valley of unstopping the wells, Isaac was stepping forward in faith in two significant ways:

First, he was reclaiming the Promises of God—that they were true and that God could be trusted to fulfill His promises. He would open those wells as a sign that he believed God's promises. Secondly, he was reclaiming his identity as a child of the Promise—that those promises were not just for his father— *they were for him*. They were *his* inheritance.

Isaac would no longer live as a passive bystander to God's promises. He claimed God's promises and his own identity as one through whom the promises of God would be realized.

෬ ෨෧ ෨

We're seeing a whole new Isaac now. Even though he has been pushed into a valley, he's not letting it defeat him. He's got a new purpose and a new focus. He's left fear behind. He's left contempt behind. He's doing the hard work that will set him up to once again thrive, both physically and spiritually. He's making some serious progress—and that's when the trouble begins.

Day Four: Quarreling and Opposition

Read Genesis 26:19-21

> *19 But when Isaac's servants dug in the valley and found there a well of spring water, 20 the herders of Gerar quarreled with Isaac's herders, saying, "The water is ours." So he called the well Esek, because they contended with him. 21 Then they dug another well, and they quarreled over that one also; so he called it Sitnah.*

* What did Isaac name the first well?

"Esek" (ay-sek) is the Hebrew word for "contention." The definition of "contention" is: *"heated disagreement; dispute; argument."*

* What did Isaac name the second well?

"Sitnah" (sit-naw) is the Hebrew word for "enmity." Take a look at what the Merriam-Webster Dictionary had to say about enmity:

> "Enmity and its synonyms hostility, animosity, and animus all indicate deep-seated dislike or ill will. Enmity (which derives from an Anglo-French word meaning "enemy") suggests true hatred, either overt or concealed. Hostility implies strong, open enmity that shows itself in attacks or aggression. Animosity carries the sense of anger, vindictiveness, and sometimes

the desire to destroy what one hates. Animus is generally less violent than animosity, but definitely conveys active prejudice or ill will."[11]

Can you see the increase of tension between the two groups by looking at the names Isaac gave the wells? First, there was contention— a heated disagreement about whose well it was. Isaac let that go. *"Fine. Have the well. You win this argument. I disagree, but you can have it. We'll dig another one."*

Based on the name he gave the second well, however, I wonder if Isaac wasn't beginning to sense that this was more than just a dispute over wells. This was active opposition— hostility directed straight at him. Perhaps Isaac sensed that no matter what he did, he would be actively opposed by this group of people. Perhaps he noticed that this wasn't about the wells; it was about preventing him from being successful. It was personal. And so Isaac named the well "enmity," "hostility," "Sitnah."

Now, here's what's interesting about this Hebrew word "Sitnah": it comes from the same Hebrew root that the word "Satan" comes from. In other words, this is the stuff of which the enemy of our souls is made. He is hostility. He is animosity. He is friction and strife, dissension and conflict. And you can bet it thrills him to have us stuck in quarreling and opposition with others. When we are swirling around in the chaos and pain of quarreling, discord, and conflict with the people around us—especially with brothers and sisters in the body of Christ— he is elated. *He knows this is one way he can steal our joy and prevent us from becoming the people God wants us to be.*

Because…

How will love flourish in us if we are constantly trapped in conflict?

How will love flourish in us if we are stressed and on guard, or if we live in a constant state of anger, bitterness, or even hatred toward someone else?

How will love flourish in our families, our communities, our churches, or the world if we are fighting and bickering about who is right and who his wrong—who the good guys are and who the bad guys are?

❧ ❧ ❧

Look again at this word "Sitnah" or "enmity." When I looked up it up, this is the way another dictionary showed it:

enmity: Middle English: from Old French **enemi(s) tie** [12]

Let your eyes just fall on that for a second. What do you see? Do you see "tied to the enemy?" As long as we continue to engage in quarreling with those who oppose us, we are in bondage, tied to our enemy.

Isaac had a choice to make: Would he continue to engage with those who actively opposed him? Isaac may have been tempted to go back to his old ways of thinking and reacting to stress—back to functioning and reacting out of fear. He may have felt the pull to dig his heels in and demand that they honor the covenant with his father, demand that they honor the work he and his servants had done, demand that they respect him, demand that he was right and they were wrong. But as long as he was entangled in quarreling and opposition with the difficult people around him he would remain stuck, distracted, and separated from the flourishing life God had for him—tied to the enemy.

☙ ✻ ❧

Let's leave Genesis for a bit and take a trip into some New Testament territory. Look up and read **Galatians 5:16-21**

* Look in verse 19 at the various "works of the flesh." Underline the ones that have to do with contentious relationships with others.

Here in this passage, the Apostle Paul names fifteen "works of the flesh." Eight of the fifteen have to do with contentious relationships with others: Enmities, strife, jealousy, anger, quarrels, dissensions, factions, envy. Then Paul says in verse 21, *"I am warning you, as I warned you before: those who do such things will not inherit the kingdom of God."*

* What do you think Paul means when he says "will not inherit the kingdom of God?"

This is a stern warning. No doubt Paul wants the believers in Galatia to sit up and listen to what he is saying and take it seriously. One thing, however, Paul is NOT saying is "you won't go to heaven." Rather, what we should understand is that whenever we engage in attitudes and behaviors like these, *the kingdom of God does not manifest in us.*

Jesus ushered in the Kingdom of God, and it is our inheritance as children of God. It's not something we receive after we die; rather, we become citizens of the kingdom now when we choose to live by God's Spirit instead of by the desires of the flesh. I keep myself out of the kingdom of God, thereby wasting my inheritance, when I choose to live by anger, enmity, jealousy, etc. These things, Paul says, are directly opposed to the Spirit of God.

In other words, when we embrace these harmful, negative attitudes, we are directly opposing the flourishing of the Kingdom of God in our lives.

Read Galatians 5:22-26

The fruit of the Spirit flourish in citizens of the Kingdom of God. These qualities are our inheritance. They are promised to become manifest in our lives when we live by the Spirit. Do you want more joy in your life? Peace? Patience? Self-control? Stop living according to the desires of your flesh, and be guided by the Spirit.

Isaac would not go back to his old ways of thinking and reacting. He would not go back to living in fear. He would not follow what his flesh may have convinced him he should do. He would move away from the quarreling and opposition to live in his promised inheritance.

Read Genesis 26:22

> [22] *He moved from there and dug another well, and they did not quarrel over it; so he called it Rehoboth, saying, "Now the Lord has made room for us, and we shall be fruitful in the land."*

"Rehoboth" (ray-ho-both) is a Hebrew word that means "Broad Places" or "Room."

What was waiting for Isaac on the other side of all that quarreling, conflict and opposition? His Rehoboth—his Broad Place—where there was plenty of room for him to be exactly who God had called him to be. He could grow; he could mature; he could be successful; he could live fully into the promises of God.

Getting Some Distance

Do you need to get some distance from some quarrelsome people or situations? Is it possible that you could be the quarrelsome person? Either way, getting some distance from arguing and fighting with others is a wise idea. Maybe you need to exit a contentious conversation or family feud. Maybe you need to avoid discussing politics with certain people. Or maybe you need to stay out of online conversations where you are engaged in quarreling and fighting, contempt even. It may be a work environment or a romantic relationship that you need to exit. When possible, sometimes we need to physically remove ourselves from certain people, places or situations.

Prayerfully consider if there are any relationships from which you need to get some distance. Be open with God and listen patiently for what He has to say to you about that.

- Are you in a situation or relationship that is toxic to your mental, spiritual, physical or emotional health? If so, name the ways this situation or relationship is having a negative impact on you.

- In what ways are you being tempted to act or react according to the flesh instead of the Spirit?

- Is there a place of enmity and quarreling from which you need to move away? If so, what is one step you might take to gain some distance?

Day Five: A Word About Spiritual Opposition and Harassment

"For our struggle is not against enemies of blood and flesh, but against the cosmic powers of this present darkness, against the spiritual forces of evil in the heavenly places. Therefore, take up the whole armor of God so that you may be able to withstand on that day, and having done everything, to stand firm."
Ephesians 6:12-13

As you, like Isaac, start to make spiritual progress and begin to gain freedom from contentious relationships and attitudes, you can expect some spiritual opposition to come your way as well. This has been the experience of many who have journeyed forward into freedom and healing with God, and it has been my experience as well. I have found that whenever I make significant progress in my faith journey, a season of spiritual harassment is not far behind.

Not too long ago I had just such an experience. The Holy Spirit led me to take an honest look at some bitterness and pain I had been holding onto and ignoring for years. He presented me with a choice: Do the hard thing and let go of pride, hurt, bitterness, and anger in order to step into freedom and joy, or hang onto it all and remain stuck, wandering around in the same land of opposition I'd been in for years, just trying to dig wells and not getting anywhere—remaining tied to the enemy. I chose to let go and begin the process of stepping into freedom. That's when the harassment began.

It started with anxiety, worry, and fear. Painful memories of the past would suddenly come to the forefront of my mind when I least expected it. I was having bad dreams and getting terrible sleep. Moodiness led to negative thoughts and some mild depression. Sadness overwhelmed me. I felt I could cry at any moment. Then, old ways of thinking and reacting began to return. I was really taken aback by that. The worst part of it was feeling like God was very distant.

In the middle of that valley experience, some words made their way to the forefront of my mind. They would run through my mind at various times of the day, always coming just when I needed them in the middle of all the chaos and noise:

"Do not submit again to a yoke of slavery."

These words are from Galatians 5:1: *"Stand firm, therefore, and do not submit again to a yoke of slavery."* They were my constant encouragement from the Holy Spirit not to give up my progress; not to go back into captivity, but, rather, to stand firm in the strength and promises of God.

You see, the enemy's objective was to have me submit again to his yoke of slavery. He had kept me in a place of wandering for years, but now I was making progress and finding freedom. This harassment was his attempt to take back my spiritual progress and keep me captive. He wanted me to retreat into old ways of thinking and old ways of reacting to stress.

Somewhere in the middle of this season of spiritual opposition, I had an overwhelming experience of God's presence. I was in my usual morning spot praying, crying, and pouring my heart out to God over the distress I was in. I opened an online devotional for the day and was astonished to see the topic: spiritual warfare and harassment. Every word seemed to be written for me in that moment, which was so comforting.

The devotional suggested we listen to the hymn *A Mighty Fortress is our God*. I clicked the link and listened. Again, every word spoke to what I was experiencing.

A mighty fortress is our God, a bulwark never failing;
Our helper he amid the flood of mortal ills prevailing.
For still our ancient foe doth seek to work us woe;
His craft and power are great, and armed with cruel hate,
On earth is not his equal.

Did we in our own strength confide, our striving would be losing,
Were not the right man on our side, the man of God's own choosing.
Dost ask who that may be? Christ Jesus it is he;
Lord Sabaoth his name, from age to age the same,
And he must win the battle.

And though this world, with devils filled,
should threaten to undo us,
We will not fear, for God hath willed his
truth to triumph through us.
The Prince of Darkness grim, we tremble not for him;
His rage we can endure, for lo, his doom is sure;
One little word shall fell him.

That word above all earthly powers, no thanks to them, abideth;
The Spirit and the gifts are ours, thru him who with us sideth.
Let goods and kindred go, this mortal life also;
The body they may kill; God's truth abideth still;
His kingdom is forever.[13]

As I listened, I was in awe. I was in awe of my God who would whisper to me, "Stand firm. Do not submit." I was in awe of my God who would send the perfect message at the perfect time to bring peace to my troubled mind and strength to my weary soul. I was overwhelmed at the thought that God would send me a song to remind me that the enemy has already lost and the kingdom I'm gaining is forever.

The song ended and I sat weeping in the silence. Then, straight into my spirit came another whisper—sweet and gentle, yet strong and sure: *"I am here."* And in that moment, I knew I would endure.

Maybe you have experienced or are experiencing some form of spiritual harassment. If so, take courage. You are not alone. Your God sees you. Your God hears you. You can endure. So, stand firm and do not submit again to a yoke of slavery.

If there is any good news regarding any spiritual harassment you face, it's this: You are making progress, and what awaits you on the other side is an even greater move of God in your life! So, stand firm to experience a depth of faith and connection with God you have not yet experienced. Stand firm, so you can see healing and restoration of your heart and mind, even your strained relationships. Stand firm, so you can see your gifts and creativity explode. Stand firm, to see God use you in ways you never imagined. There is no limit to what God can do in you and through you! So, stand firm, trust God and do not submit again to a yoke of slavery.

↶ ✤ ↷

Read Genesis 26:23-25

> [23] *From there he went up to Beer-sheba.* [24] *And that very night the Lord appeared to him and said, "I am the God of your father Abraham; do not be afraid, for I am with you and will bless you and make your offspring numerous for my servant Abraham's sake."* [25] *So he built an altar there, called on the name of the Lord, and pitched his tent there. And there Isaac's servants dug a well.*

In the midst of this valley experience, God lovingly spoke again to Isaac and reminded him what was true: *I will fulfill my purposes for your life. I've said it once, and I'll say it a thousand times more. Do not be afraid. You are mine. I am with you.* This is where Isaac would now settle and begin to dig deep—in God's presence.

The amazing progress Isaac made all started because he first chose to claim the promises of God and begin living like the child of the promise he was. These are the steps we must also take if we are to reclaim joy.

- What promises of God do you need to claim for your life?

- In what ways do you need to begin living into your identity as a child of the promise?

Week 3 – Reclaiming Joy in the Face of Bitterness and Unforgiveness

Day One: A Blast From the Past

Isaac is in his "broad place." There is finally room for him to become the man he needs to be. There is room for him to thrive and be fruitful. He has moved away from the contentious relationships with the Philistines, no longer living in daily conflict and opposition. He's had a deeply influential experience with God at Beersheba, where God reiterated His promises reminding Isaac not to fear, that He was with him and that He would fulfill his purposes for his life. Life is good for Isaac. He's a new man and it is clear that the blessings of God are all over his life. It was so obvious that even Abimelech noticed.

Read **Genesis 26:26-29**

> ²⁶ *Then Abimelech went to him from Gerar, with Ahuzzath his adviser and Phicol the commander of his army.* ²⁷ *Isaac said to them, "Why have you come to me, seeing that you hate me and have sent me away from you?"* ²⁸ *They said, "We see plainly that the Lord has been with you; so we say, let there be an oath between you and us, and let us make a covenant with you* ²⁹ *so that you will do us no harm, just as we have not touched you and have done to you nothing but*

*good and have sent you away in peace. You are now
the blessed of the Lord."*

Have you ever had this happen? You've moved on from a contentious relationship, found some peace and some space to live and breathe and become without all the quarreling and fighting, when someone from that contentious past shows back up or reaches out in some way?

- If you've had that happen, write down some adjectives to describe your initial reaction. (Shock, anger, fear, etc.)

- Look at verse 27. What was the first thing out of Isaac's mouth when he saw Abimelech and his men? Write it below in your own words.

Does it sound like Isaac is ready to treat Abimelech and his men with kindness? Does he sound happy to see them? Isaac's words of "welcome" are a little lacking in hospitality. Even though Isaac has made significant progress, I wonder if we're not hearing a little bit of pain and baggage from the past. Let's see how this is going to play out.

- **Look back at verses 28-29 at Abimelech's response to Isaac's question.** What do you think about how Abimelech framed his request to make peace with Isaac, especially the phrase, "*...just as we have not touched you and have done to you nothing but good and have sent you away in peace?*" Do you think this is an accurate statement based on their past relationship? Why or why not?

Again, as in the past, Isaac had some options in front of him.

- Make a list of what you think Isaac's options were concerning how he could respond to these men.

Here are some I came up with:

- Argue with them about the exact nature of the past and try to be right.
- Blame them for the past and claim that he is the victim.
- Hang on to the past, remain bitter, and refuse to make peace.
- Let go of the past and agree to a covenant of peace.

Regardless of whether or not Abimelech's account of the past was completely accurate, what's important was that he was reaching out to Isaac to make peace—not to be his best friend, not to live as next-door neighbors, join the same book club, or get coffee every morning—but to say, *"Let's put the past behind us and commit to do no more harm."* Abimelech made the first move, and now it was Isaac's choice about how to respond.

Read **Genesis 26:30-31**

> [30] *So he made them a feast, and they ate and drank.* [31]
> *In the morning they rose early and exchanged oaths;*
> *and Isaac set them on their way, and they departed*
> *from him in peace.*

Our man, Isaac, choose to do what love would do. He prepared a meal for them, and then they sat down and ate together, each of them letting go of the past so it could no longer hold them in bondage. Then they parted in peace.

Isaac had unstopped Abraham's wells, which was crucial work because it showed that he was placing his faith in God's promises and claiming his identity and inheritance as a child of the promise. This encounter with Abimelech revealed that Isaac had some additional wells to unstop. He needed to open the wells inside of his heart, mind, and soul through forgiveness and making peace with Abimelech.

⌒ ꙮ ⌒

Years back I had an experience similar to Isaac's. I was sitting at my kitchen table working on a sermon for the following Sunday, when I received a message from someone I hadn't seen in a while, someone I had a rather contentious past with. I had distanced myself from the relationship, which was the right move. I was in a new space in my life where I was truly thriving, where God's blessings were quite tangible, and where I was feeling the freest and most confident I'd ever felt. Even though I was in my "Broad Place" surrounded by so many blessings, I continued to carry a lot of hurt, bitterness, and anger over the past.

I believe now that the kind and complimentary message was this person's version of, *"I see clearly that God is with you."* An offer of peace was being extended to me, presenting me with a choice: unstop the wells, or remain stuck in bitterness and anger.

My initial reaction was very similar to Isaac's: *"What are you doing messaging me and saying nice things to me? You hate me, remember?"* I wanted to roll my eyes (*ahem*...contempt!), close the message, and never look at it again. But just as quickly as that emotion rose up in me and that thought crossed my mind, I sensed God speaking straight into my spirit addressing that ugly attitude. *"Susan, you can't be an ass in your Broad Place."* (I didn't know God would say "ass", but you know what they say: "If the shoe fits!")

This correction was so intense that it jolted me out of my bad attitude. Immediately, I was convicted because I knew what was true: I was flourishing. God was with me and God had been blessing me in abundant ways. I had nothing to be angry about. There was nothing God was withholding from me. If I held on to that anger and refused to make peace with someone who was reaching out to me in kindness, it would be an insult to the grace and kindness God has continually shown me in the face of my many shortcomings and failures, as well as the many things I did to contribute to the brokenness of that relationship.

I also realized that my responsibility wasn't to make an assessment concerning the genuineness of the gesture or to give my account of the past. My responsibility in that moment was to respond with kindness, and with as much love as I could, so that is what I did.

This may sound so elementary to you, but please understand that even small responses of kindness in love are extremely difficult when you have nursed anger and bitterness for so long. With my heart racing, I *chose* to do what love would do even though I didn't *feel* loving at the time. I made a conscious choice in that moment to be a woman of love, not a woman of bitterness and anger.

Do you remember what I mentioned in week two about the freedom I stepped into when God led me to do the hard work of forgiveness? This was the start of that journey. This one choice for love as I sat at my kitchen table set me up for a flood of the Spirit in my soul.

In the week following that choice, God started doing a significant work of healing in my life. A spiritual stronghold of anger left me during this healing process. I felt the impact of that release physically, emotionally, and spiritually. My heart was finally opened up to forgiveness—real, true, forgiveness.

After I forgave this person, a list of names flooded my mind—a list of people that I needed to forgive. I had no idea I was holding on to so much bitterness. But, you see, with the anger gone, there was nothing for bitterness to cling to, and forgiveness was so much easier to embrace and enact. Through the act of forgiveness, I moved into a brand-new spiritual space as the Holy Spirit flooded my heart and mind with His presence in a profound way. I haven't been the same since.

⌒ ʊ̈ɛ ↻

Perhaps you need to have your own "kitchen table" moment. Prayerfully consider if there is anyone from your present or past that you are harboring bitterness, anger, or resentment against. With this person or people in mind, move mindfully through this guided prayer.

Begin by taking a moment of silence to reflect and listen. Take slow, deep breaths and then exhale slowly and intentionally. You may imagine with every inhale that you are breathing in the Spirit of God, and with every exhale you are expelling negative attitudes and thoughts. Continue this breathing practice throughout the rest of the exercise.

⌒ ʊ̈ɛ ↻

Lord, may your Holy Spirit override the negative leanings of my spirit. May you lead every thought, every emotion, every word, every attitude. I confess to you my attitudes of _____
against _____. *I ask that you forgive me for these negative attitudes.*

Silence

51

Lord, I ask that you fill me with your love. May the spirit of anger be driven away through the power of your love.

Silence

I confess that I have not been considering making peace, Lord, and that I have been desiring my own version of vengeance. What I really prefer is to live in peace. Give me your courage and your peace-making abilities. May I not be defensive. May I not be angry. May I look at _____ through your eyes of love.

Silence

May I be silent until your Spirit gives me the words I need to speak at the right time. Guard my words. I surrender to you. I do not need to be right. I will not let pride and anger lead in this situation/ relationship. Lead me forward in your love, and may your Spirit rest on _____ today.

Silence

Give _____ a sense of your love and peace. Open my eyes to see _____ how you see him/her. Open his/her eyes to see me how you see me as well. Open our eyes to each other in your Spirit of Love.

Amen.

Day Two: Hidden Anger

One of the most astonishing "wake-up calls" I had during this healing process was the awareness of how much anger I had been walking around with. I had no idea how angry I had been until it was gone. In reality, I had been living with a lot of hidden anger. I say "hidden" even though it probably wasn't hidden very well.

What is hidden anger? Hidden anger comes out when you least expect it. When you have hidden anger, you find that you are angry in situations where you shouldn't be—small things get you more agitated than they should. You react to people and situations instead of responding.

- Have you ever noticed yourself reacting in angry ways that didn't match the situation? If so, name some of the things that tend to "set you off."

Look up and read Ephesians 4:25-5:2

- Look at verses 26 & 27. Who does Paul say we are making room for when we hang on to anger?

- Look carefully over the entire passage and make a list of everything Paul says to put away or give up.

- Look at verses 4:32-5:2. Write down the traits and/or actions Paul says we should possess.

- Looking at both lists, which traits are more prevalent in your life right now?

- Look at verses 5:1-2. Who does Paul say we are imitating when we treat others these ways?

- Look in verse 5:2 and circle the phrase "live in love."

We have no idea the damage we are doing to ourselves and the people around us when we hang on to anger and bitterness and nurse grudges from the past. We have no idea what abundance of the Spirit we are missing out on when we cling to all that garbage. Paul says we are actually making room for the devil when we hang on to anger. That thought alone should give us pause.

The lie we buy too often is that hanging on to anger and bitterness is going to make us feel better and satisfy us in the long run. Perhaps it's satisfying in the moment, but as we've already seen, it is toxic to our bodies, our minds, our souls and our relationships with others. Hanging on to anger robs us of joy, peace, patience, kindness and all the other qualities and fruit of the Spirit. We must choose what kind of people we will be. Will we live in bitterness or will we live in love?

- Ask yourself, "Based on my current attitudes, who am I making room for in my soul?"

- What is one practical step you can take today to live in love?

Day Three: The Current of God's Love

"Jesus said, 'Love your enemies,' and I take that to include a promise that the burden of hatred and enmity can be lifted from me toward that person. He also said 'Forgive.' That, too, is a promise that I can escape the burden of unforgiveness. He will help me do that." —
Dallas Willard, *Life Without Lack*

If you have ever done any kayaking or rafting, or even if you've sat in an inner tube and floated down a lazy river at a waterpark, you understand the nature of a current. Currents are constantly moving forward. A current is going somewhere with intentionality, and if you're in it, you're going with it.

God is very much like a current. He is constantly moving forward to have His will accomplished. He is a powerful force Who changes the landscape of this world through the transformation of our hearts and minds. We are invited to step into the current of His transforming love with him, and partner with the Holy Spirit to change the landscape of this world.

Stepping into that current with God is exhilarating! When we are flowing with him, our gifts are built up, our love increases, and our boundaries are expanded. We find joy and fulfillment from being near to God and being a part of the significant things that He is about. But when we try to go against that current, or stand still and remain unmoved by the current of His love, we soon find that we are uncomfortable, exhausted, and just plain unsuccessful.

Jonah is a great example of someone who tried to go against the current of God's love. Jonah was a prophet of Israel who chose to remain unchanged in his heart, stubbornly digging his heels in, refusing to let the current of God's love move him or transform him.

You see, Jonah had some deep bitterness and hatred against a group of people called the Assyrians. He decided that they were evil and cruel, and you know what: he wasn't completely wrong. They had a terrible reputation for treating other nations with severe cruelty. Because of that, Jonah would not desire anything good for them. When God called him to go speak to the Assyrians on His behalf, Jonah refused. He knew that God is love, that God shows mercy, and that God forgives—those were the last things he wanted for the Assyrians.

Jonah ran away, attempting to go against the current of God's will. When he finally went to the Assyrians as instructed, they responded to his message and repented of their sins. Just as Jonah feared, God relented from punishing them. But instead of letting the current of God's love flow through him and taking joy in such a miraculous event, Jonah remained bitter and angry.

Look up and read Jonah 4:1-11

• What strikes you about Jonah's attitude?

• How would you describe Jonah based on these verses?

• How does this attitude make you feel about Jonah?

• Have you ever been like Jonah? If so, when and how?

Jonah didn't want the Assyrians to receive God's grace and

forgiveness. He would have rather repaid evil for evil. We don't want to be like Jonah. We want to be people who willingly step into the current of God's love to bring the good news of God's grace, mercy, and forgiveness to everyone.

ᖓ ᘯᓱᕪ ᖇ

The baptismal liturgy of the United Methodist Church contains beautiful baptismal vows. Take a look at the first vow:

"Do you renounce the spiritual forces of wickedness,
reject the evil powers of this world,
and repent of your sin?"[14]

What does it look like to renounce the spiritual forces of wickedness and reject the evil powers of this world? Well, it looks like what the Apostle Paul described in Romans 12.

Look up and read Romans 12:9-21

- Which of these instructions resonates the most with you? Why?

- Which of these are the most difficult for you? Why?

Focus on verses 19 & 20

These verses can be confusing because we don't understand this phrase about heaping burning coals on someone's head. Paul is quoting Proverbs 25:21-22. According to an article by the Engedi Resource Center, "this saying in Proverbs is in the middle of several other proverbs that use physical images to describe emotional reactions."[15] These verses compare the physical discomfort of having burning coals on your head to the emotional discomfort an enemy will feel when you waken his conscience about his poor conduct toward you by showing kindness to him in the face of his unkindness.

We will not transform the world around us or build God's Kingdom by partnering with the spiritual forces of wickedness through seeking revenge, hanging on to bitterness, or withholding good from people. We will transform the world by living in love and showing kindness in the face of another's unkindness. Consider these words from Barnes' Notes on the Bible:

> *The way to promote "peace" is to do good even to enemies. The way to bring a man to repentance is to do him good. On this principle God is acting continually. He does good to all, even to the rebellious; and he designs that his goodness should lead people to repentance. People will resist wrath, anger, and power; but "goodness" they cannot resist; it finds its way to the heart; and the conscience does its work, and the sinner is overwhelmed at the remembrance of his crimes.*
>
> *If people would act on the principles of the gospel, the world would soon be at peace. No man would suffer himself many times to be overwhelmed in this way with coals of fire. It is not human nature...and if Christians would meet all unkindness with kindness, all malice with benevolence, and all wrong with right, peace would soon pervade the community, and even opposition to the gospel might soon die away.*[16]

- Write down the name(s) of a person or people with whom you need to practice Romans 12:9-21.

- Name some practical ways you can show kindness to a difficult person or in a difficult situation this week.

- Come back to this page later and write down what you noticed in yourself, in others, or the situation as a result of your choice for kindness.

Day Four: Retaining v/s Forgiving

Look up and read John 20:19-23

These verses confused me for years. I couldn't get what Jesus was saying to his disciples because, for some reason, I always heard Jesus' words a little bit like this:

> *Receive the Holy Spirit. You now have the authority to forgive sins like I do. So, Peter, if you decide that Joe Shmo's sins should be forgiven, then I support that decision. But, if you decide that Joe Shmo's sins are just too gross and horrible, then you don't have to forgive his sins.*

I knew this didn't work theologically, and I knew it didn't match the character of God, but it sounded to me like Jesus was giving them the option to withhold forgiveness at certain times. It all just confused me. So for years, I did what most of us do when we come across something we don't understand in Scripture: I moved past it and acted like it wasn't there.

This year during Lent I was reading through the Gospel of John. When I reached these verses in John 20, I had an epiphany. Jesus wasn't giving the disciples a special privilege to choose NOT to forgive. **Jesus was telling them how crucial forgiveness is to the transformation of the world!**

Focus again on John 20:23.

> *"Receive the Holy Spirit. If you forgive the sins of any, they are forgiven them; if you retain the sins of any, they are retained."*

When you retain the sins of others—remaining angry, bitter, vengeful, etc.—the spiritual forces of wickedness still have power over you and those relationships. Refusing to forgive brings brokenness, sickness, and death into our bodies, minds, and souls. That brokenness affects my other relationships and continues until its evil effects bleed into the community.

Forgiveness BREAKS that power.

You see, God has already chosen not to retain our sins. He has chosen to forgive us. So, when we choose to step into that current and forgive others as he forgave, sin has no more power, because God has already done the ultimate work of forgiving.

Because of God's ultimate act of forgiveness through Jesus Christ, our forgiveness of another now has greater power. Because once we release the sins of others that we have been retaining, the remaining vestiges of power the enemy sought to have over us are defeated, and forgiveness has its full effect.

Tom Oden said in his book *Life in the Spirit*, "*God not only forgives sin through the son, but through the Spirit works to overturn the power of sin in actual daily interpersonal behavior and life in community.*"[17] We have the power within us, through the Holy Spirit, to actually overturn the power of sin in our daily lives through forgiveness! Is it any wonder, then, why we come up against so much opposition when it comes to forgiving others? Through forgiveness, we can actually undo the work of the enemy and transform the world!

But forgiveness is not easy, friends. Forgiveness flies in the face of our natural human inclination to pride and self-protection. Sometimes even the thought of forgiving makes us sick and angry all over again. This, again, is why it is so critical that we choose to be men and women sourced by love. We must create an environment in our souls that is inhospitable to hate, anger, and bitterness. We must lean into everything God is and ask Him repeatedly to fill us up with His Spirit. We must choose to die to pride and being right in order to live in freedom and abundant joy.

Death is never easy. Death always hurts. And depending on what you have been holding on to and how long you have nurtured it, dying to those things can take some time. But your God has all the time you need. He is not going anywhere.

And remember, He is not condemning you. He understands your pain. Do you hear that? God understands YOUR pain. He was there when the hurt happened. His heart broke when your heart broke. But it also grieves him when you carry around in your body, mind, and soul something that will only bring death. Let it go. The anger, the bitterness... they're not your friends. Trust God to replace the pain with His healing and His joy. You can do it.

• What sins of others have you been retaining?

- What has been the result of that? How has it affected you...

  Physically

  Emotionally

  Spiritually

- What will you choose to forgive today? Start small if you need to. Practice makes perfect. ☺

Day Five: A Source of Healing for the World

Let's go back to Genesis now and look at what happened after Isaac made his choice for love and made peace with Abimelech.

Read **Genesis 26:32**

> ³² *That same day Isaac's servants came and told him about the well that they had dug, and said to him, "We have found water!"*

On the same day Isaac made peace with Abimelech, his servants came to him and reported, "We have found water!" The well they had been digging had finally hit the source. Fresh, clean, nourishing water was flowing into the well!

That is a beautiful picture of what was going on spiritually within Isaac. Once Isaac chose to make peace with Abimelech, Isaac's heart tapped into the source of love, and the living water of the Holy Spirit was able to flood into his heart in a new and fresh way.

The same is true for us. The living water of the Holy Spirit will flow into us when we not only move away from quarreling, bitterness and anger, but when we **forgive** those who have hurt us and make peace with the people with whom we have a past.[3] If we want to experience true abundance, if we want more of the Spirit of God at work in our lives, if we want a move of God to happen in and through us in an exponential way, we must

---

[3] Reconciliation with another is not always possible. Some situations like abuse, for instance, may require that you remain distant from your perpetrator. However, many of our disputes with others are not the result of dangerous abuse. Having said that, I do believe we can still make peace, even with the people who have abused us, by making peace in our own souls and our attitudes toward them. We can choose forgiveness even when reconciliation is not possible.

unstop the wells and RECLAIM FORGIVENESS, making room in our hearts for the living water of God's Spirit to flow.

Look up Ezekiel 47:1-12

Read verses 1-2

- In this vision, what did Ezekiel see flowing out of the temple?

- What do you think the water represents?

The water represents the Holy Spirit. Ezekiel's vision is a beautiful picture of the Holy Spirit flowing out from the Presence of God.

Read verses 3-6

- What do you notice about the water?

The more Ezekiel moved through the water, the more the water increased and enveloped him. At first, it was ankle-deep, then deep enough to swim in, then it was a river too wide to even cross!

This is what happens in our lives when we choose to step into the living waters of the Holy Spirit. As we begin our journey of faith, we're ankle-deep with God and His Spirit. As we continue to journey with Him, He invites us to go deeper still—to live less and less by our selfish desires and more and more according to His, to offer kindness to those who don't deserve it and to forgive others as He has forgiven us. We won't live this way if we choose to remain in control only going ankle-deep in our journey with the Holy Spirit. But when we choose to keep walking out into the deep waters, pretty soon we'll find that the Spirit is capable of doing beautiful things in and through us that we never thought were possible.

Read verses 6-9

• Where did Ezekiel's "guide" lead him?

• What did Ezekiel see along the bank?

• What did Ezekiel's guide say would be the result of this flowing river?

• Circle the phrase "...*everything will live where the river goes.*"

Holding on to anger and bitterness and nurturing fear and contempt bring sickness into our lives. Refusing to forgive and refusing to make peace bring dryness—a desert. It's hard to thrive in a desert. Let the living waters of the Holy Spirit flood into every aspect of your life because, as it says here in Ezekiel, "everything lives where the river goes." Everywhere the Spirit covers you, there will be life.

Read Verses 10-12

• What kind of fruit will the trees on the bank of this river bear?

Will the trees ever wither? Will their fruit ever fail? No, they will never fail, because the living water flowing directly from the Presence of God is the source of their life.

• Look at the last sentence in verse 12 and write it here.

These trees, whose lives are being sourced by the river flowing straight out of the Presence of God, become a source of sustenance and healing. **This is the life God intends for each of us**—that we would be sourced by the living water of His Spirit and our lives would bring joy, delight, nourishment and healing to the world. This is where our joy comes from! Joy is not something we create or find—it is something that is given to us from the Spirit.

God has promised us the kingdom. He has promised us the beautiful inheritance of His Spirit. He has promised us a life full of abundance and joy. He boldly proclaims that he can turn us into people who bring healing and reconciliation into this world. So may you let go. May you step in. May you go out into the deep with God. And may your life be a source of healing for the world. Amen and Amen.

> *"May the God of peace himself sanctify you entirely;*
> *and may your spirit and soul and body be kept sound*
> *and blameless at the coming of our Lord Jesus Christ.*
> *The one who calls you is faithful, and he will do this."*
> *~ 1 Thessalonians 5:23-24*

Endnotes

1 Arthur C. Brooks, *Love Your Enemies* (New York, NY: Broadside Books, 2019), 22

2 Brooks, 26

3 Brooks, 25

4 Brooks, 25

5 Kirsten Weir, "The Pain of Social Rejection," American Psychological Association, Monitor on Psychology 43, no. 4 (Apr. 2012), 50, http://www.apa.org/monitor/2012/04/rejection.aspx

6 Brooks, 23

7 Dallas Willard, *Life Without Lack: Living in the Fullness of Psalm 23* (Nashville, TN: Thomas Nelson, 2018), 159

8 Willard, 170

9 https://www.dictionary.com/browse/valley

10 Marvin E Tate, Word Biblical Commentary: Psalms 51-100 (Dallas, TX: Word Books, 1990), 362

11 https://www.merriam-webster.com/dictionary/enmity

12 https://www.google.com/search/enmity

13 Martin Luther, *A Mighty Fortress is Our God*, 1529

14 *The United Methodist Book of Worship* (Nashville, TN: The United Methodist Publishing House, 1992), 88

15 Tverberg, L. (2006). Heaping Burning Coals? Hebraic Insight on Puzzling Passages [Article]. http://www.engediresourcecenter.com/URL

16 Albert Barnes, *Notes on the Bible* [1834]

17 Thomas Oden, *Life in the Spirit* (New York, NY: Harper Collins, 1992), 4

Printed in the United States
By Bookmasters